Colors of the
NAVAJO

by Emily Abbink
illustrations by Janice Lee Porter

COLORS
OF THE WORLD

Carolrhoda Books, Inc. / Minneapolis

To the Navajo People—EA
For Jeannie—JLP

The publisher wishes to thank Irene Silentman, Navajo Language Project at the Navajo Nation for all her help with the preparation of this book. Thanks also go to native speakers Mae Austin and Gloria Emerson.

Map on page 3 by John Erste

Copyright © 1998 by Carolrhoda Books, Inc.

This book is available in two editions:
Library binding by Carolrhoda Books, Inc.
Soft cover by First Avenue Editions
c/o The Lerner Publishing Group
241 First Avenue North
Minneapolis, MN 55401 U.S.A.

Website address: www.lernerbooks.com

Library of Congress Cataloging-in-Publication Data
Abbink, Emily.
 Colors of the Navajo / by Emily Abbink ; illustrations by Janice
Lee Porter.
  p.   cm. — (Colors of the world)
 Includes index
 Summary: Uses colors to focus on the history, culture, and
physical surroundings of the Navajo Indians.
 ISBN 1-57505-207-5 (alk. paper)
 ISBN 1-57505-269-5 (pbk.)
 1. Navajo Indians—Juvenile literature. 2. Colors—Juvenile
literature. [1. Navajo Indians. 2. Indians of North America—
Southwest, New. 3. Color.] I. Porter, Janice Lee, ill.
II. Title. III. Series.
E99.N3A17   1998
979'.004972—dc21   97-26013

Manufactured in the United States of America
1 2 3 4 5 6 – SP – 03 02 01 00 99 98

Introduction

Navajos are Native Americans who have lived in the southwestern United States for over five hundred years. Most Navajos live on or near the Navajo Indian Reservation. A reservation is a piece of land set aside by the federal government for Native Americans. The Navajo Indian Reservation is the biggest U.S. reservation, in both population and land area. It includes parts of New Mexico, Arizona, and Utah.

Some reservation Navajos follow traditional Navajo occupations—they herd sheep, weave, and make jewelry. But more and more Navajos work for mining companies, schools, or the government, while others move off the reservation to work in nearby cities or towns. Balancing Navajo culture with American technology can be extremely difficult.

Turquoise

Dootł'izhii (doe-thl-ih-zhee)

Tap, tap, tap. Using a tiny hammer, a silversmith carefully nudges a smooth, **turquoise** oval into a silver bracelet setting. Gently, he hammers the silver band tightly around the turquoise to secure the stone. Finished, he polishes both turquoise and silver until they gleam in the sun.

During the 1700s and 1800s, Navajos learned silversmithing from Spanish settlers. With melted silver coins, the Navajos made beautiful, heavy jewelry to display their wealth. By combining their ideas with those of the neighboring Pueblo Indians and Spanish people, the Navajos developed their own style. Turquoise surrounded by silver was the most popular of all.

Navajos traded their handmade jewelry for food, clothes, and tools. Around 1900, tourists began to buy Navajo bracelets, necklaces, and rings. Many Navajos continue to make and sell elegant turquoise jewelry, which is prized by collectors around the world.

Brown

Dinilzhin (dih-nil-zhin)

Traditionally, Navajos lived in **brown** hogans (ho-GAHNZ), built far apart to allow room for sheep to graze between them. Easily constructed, the one-room hogans were ideal homes for people moving frequently after their herds. Most reservation Navajos still build an old-style hogan near their modern homes for ceremonies or guests.

Hogans are round, usually 25 to 30 feet across, and made of logs or stone. Brown mud plaster keeps the hogans cool in summer and warm in winter. Doorways face east, to honor the dawn. To Navajos, a hogan represents the universe, the harmony of people, the Earth, and the sky. Four main posts support the hogan's roof, or sky. The floor is Mother Earth. Between sky and Earth all living things are found.

7

8

Red

Łichíí' (thlih-chee)

Red anthills can be found nearly everywhere on the reservation. Navajos believe ants are messengers between the Earth's surface and the holy worlds below. Children learn early not to harm ants or anthills, because the spirits of angry ants might send illness.

If a child accidentally destroys an ant or anthill, a Red Antway Ceremony might be performed to cure the child. A medicine man makes a sand painting in the family's hogan. A sand painting is a design made from sand and other dry materials. The medicine man trickles thin lines of colored sand, pollen, and crushed charcoal on the dirt floor to form a dry painting of the ancient Red Ant People. Once completed, the painting is thought to be alive.

Family is invited to the ceremony. The child who harmed the ant or anthill sits on the sand painting. The medicine man invites the Red Ant People to listen to his song about the first Red Ant People. Through the sand painting, the Red Ant People send healing into the child's body. Illness flows out of the child's body and is absorbed by the sand. Before sunset, the medicine man scoops up the sand painting and carries it away from the hogan. He offers the sand back to Mother Earth with prayers. The Red Ant People are no longer angry, and the child will soon get well.

10

Yellow

Łitso (thlih-tso)

A young Navajo boy squints down the road, watching for his **yellow** school bus. He carries his homework in his backpack. He hops from foot to foot, swinging his catcher's mitt and shivering in the chilly morning. His long, dark shadow hops too.

In the early 1900s, most Navajo children were forced into boarding schools, where they slept, ate, and learned lessons. The boarding schools were set up by missionaries and the federal government to make Navajos learn the white people's way of life. Children received American names, clothes, and new, strange foods to eat. White teachers punished students who spoke Navajo. Many Navajo children got sick and died at these schools.

By the 1950s, many boarding schools for Native Americans were beginning to shut down. Navajo children could live at home with their families and take the bus to and from school. By the 1990s, students at some schools learn Navajo and English from Navajo teachers. They may also study Navajo legends, U.S. history, and native plant uses, and learn to use computers.

Suddenly, the young Navajo boy spots the yellow school bus, bouncing over washboard roads. The bus rattles to a stop in a cloud of dust. He picks a seat next to his friend. The groaning bus turns and heads toward school.

12

Black

Łizhin (thlih-zhin)

A flat piece of land, **black** with trees, rises abruptly from the surrounding desert in northeast Arizona. This formation, called Black Mesa (MAY-sah), is a familiar landmark to the Navajos. From the air, the mesa looks like a huge, outstretched hand, about seventy miles across. Black Mesa is one of the mountains sacred to both Navajos and Hopis, and it is famous for its black coal. Long ago, Navajos began to mine the coal for heating. More recently, Navajos have rented the land to power companies. Nearby generating stations turn the coal into electricity.

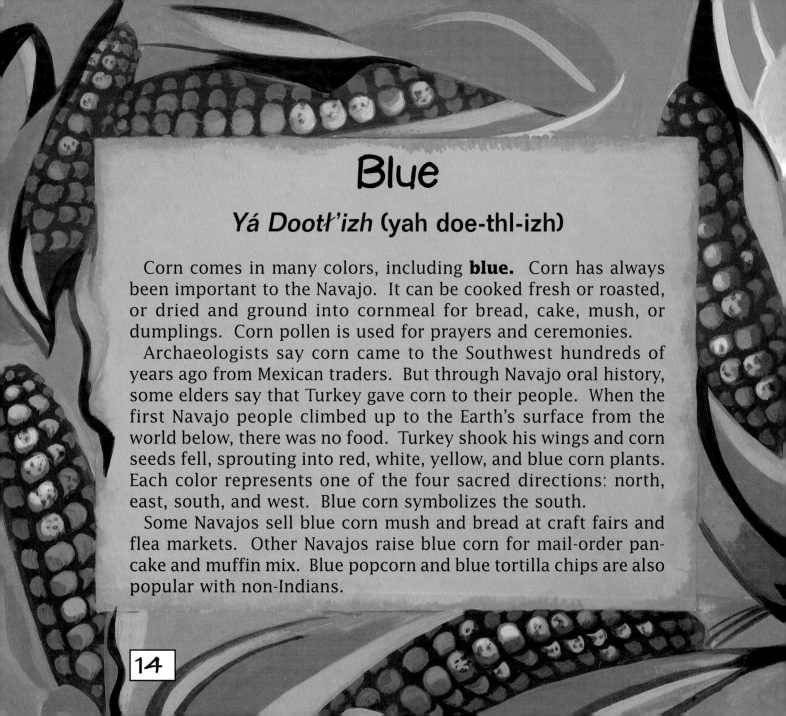

Blue

Yá Dootł'izh (yah doe-thl-izh)

Corn comes in many colors, including **blue.** Corn has always been important to the Navajo. It can be cooked fresh or roasted, or dried and ground into cornmeal for bread, cake, mush, or dumplings. Corn pollen is used for prayers and ceremonies.

Archaeologists say corn came to the Southwest hundreds of years ago from Mexican traders. But through Navajo oral history, some elders say that Turkey gave corn to their people. When the first Navajo people climbed up to the Earth's surface from the world below, there was no food. Turkey shook his wings and corn seeds fell, sprouting into red, white, yellow, and blue corn plants. Each color represents one of the four sacred directions: north, east, south, and west. Blue corn symbolizes the south.

Some Navajos sell blue corn mush and bread at craft fairs and flea markets. Other Navajos raise blue corn for mail-order pancake and muffin mix. Blue popcorn and blue tortilla chips are also popular with non-Indians.

Green

Tátł'id Dootł'izh (tah-thl-id doe-thl-izh)

Many people think nothing **green** grows in the desert. But after the winter snow melts, much of the desert turns green. Wild plants grow here and there, sprouting from cracks in the rocks and in dried earth. For centuries, Navajos have gathered and used these plants for food, medicine, dyeing wool, soap, and religious ceremonies. For example, cooked red cactus fruit makes a jelly or a sweet drink. Young, green sage leaves make medicines: breathing hot sage vapors clears a stuffy nose, and drinking sage tea cures a headache. In August, Navajos pick the ripe, green fruit that grows on yucca plants. The fruit is then cooked, dried, and stored for later use. The roots from this plant can be crushed to make a sudsy shampoo. Navajos carefully gather pollen from green corn plants for prayers and ceremonies.

Acres of green alfalfa ripple atop the mesas near Farmington in northwestern New Mexico. Here the Navajos started a huge scientific farming program. San Juan River water irrigates these farms. Fields of wheat, corn, beans, potatoes, and fruit trees provide food and jobs for Navajo people. As you can see, the desert is greener than most people think!

18

Tan

Diniiltsxóóh (dih-neel-tskho)

Canyon de Chelly's (duh SHAYZ) **tan** sandstone canyons form deep, twisting mazes. The canyon is located in northeast Arizona. For years, Navajos raided crops and livestock from Pueblo and Spanish settlers and then hid among the canyon's winding cliffs.

In 1851, the U.S. Army built Fort Defiance to stop Navajo raids on settlers. Unable to stop them, the soldiers shot Navajo horses and sheep grazing nearby. Angered, a large Navajo group attacked Fort Defiance in 1860. Most of the group then escaped into the cliffs and crevices of Canyon de Chelly. But soldiers hunted down and killed many Navajos.

Some Navajos were captured alive and taken as prisoners. The army forced them three hundred miles east to a prison camp at Fort Sumner, New Mexico. Navajos call this march "The Long Walk." Sickness and starvation killed hundreds along the way. Crowded and mistreated at the prison camp, the Navajos longed for their canyon homeland. After four long, miserable years, they were allowed to return to their homeland near Canyon de Chelly's tan cliffs.

Gray

Łibá (thlih-bah)

A young girl watches her grandmother weave a patterned **gray** wool rug. Grandmother threads her shuttle stick, wound with wool, between the loom's upright strings, beating the gray wool down securely with a wood fork. Row by row, the weaving grows—tight and even.

For many years, Navajos have woven wool from sheep they herd. Different parts of the reservation create different styles of rugs. Some rugs are made from wool that has been dyed bright colors. Grandmother makes a rug with geometric patterns using wool in its natural colors: gray, white, brown, and black. This style of rug is known as a Two Gray Hills. In the early 1900s, tourists began to buy Navajo rugs. Styles with specific colors and designs developed in different areas of the reservation. Some of these styles, like the Two Gray Hills, sell for high prices in places such as New York, Los Angeles, and Europe.

Gold

Óola (oh-lah)

Gold medals hanging around the necks of Navajo war veterans flash in the sun as the veterans proudly march in a Memorial Day parade. Navajo soldiers earned many medals for their bravery and skill during World War II. When Japanese planes bombed Pearl Harbor in 1941, hundreds of young Navajo men lined up to enlist in the armed services.

Navajo men were trained for the marines. In addition, they used their native language to devise a secret code to use against the enemy. Soon, many Navajo marines used the code system in combat against the Japanese. These coded messages were never cracked by the Japanese. Using Navajo terms such as *ayęęzhii* (meaning egg in English) for *bomb,* the Navajo code-talkers sent battle plans by radio all over the South Pacific.

Since World War II, Navajos have continued to earn gold medals for their bravery in the Armed Forces. But the code-talkers will always be remembered for their contributions to World War II. A large code-talker monument was raised in Phoenix, Arizona, in 1989 to honor these Navajo marines.

Index